AF413659

LIGHT IN DARKNESS

REFLECTIONS ON MENTAL HEALTH

BY GABRIELLE REECE

DEDICATION

To my therapists who continued to encourage me to keep writing, my dad who never stopped believing in me, and to the beautiful angels Maddie & Tuffy that I call best friends. Thank you for being my light in the darkness.

CONTENTS

INTRODUCTION

These are poems encompassing all the ups and downs of my mental health journey. Navigating my mental health has been a journey and one that I know I will be on for the rest of my time here on earth. Some days it seems okay and other days it seems unbearable. I wanted to share these poems hoping that those reading would feel heard and validated in their feelings. The world can be a scary place. There are those out there who are hurting and just want to feel heard and loved and just want to be okay even for a day.

Trigger Warning: These poems tackle different topics such as self-harm, suicidal thoughts, addiction, and different forms of trauma. Take care of yourself and stop reading if it becomes too much for you.

PART I

THE DARKNESS

*"I buried my head under the darkness
of the pillow and pretended it was
night. I couldn't see the point of
getting up. I had nothing to look
forward to."*
— Sylvia Plath, The Bell Jar

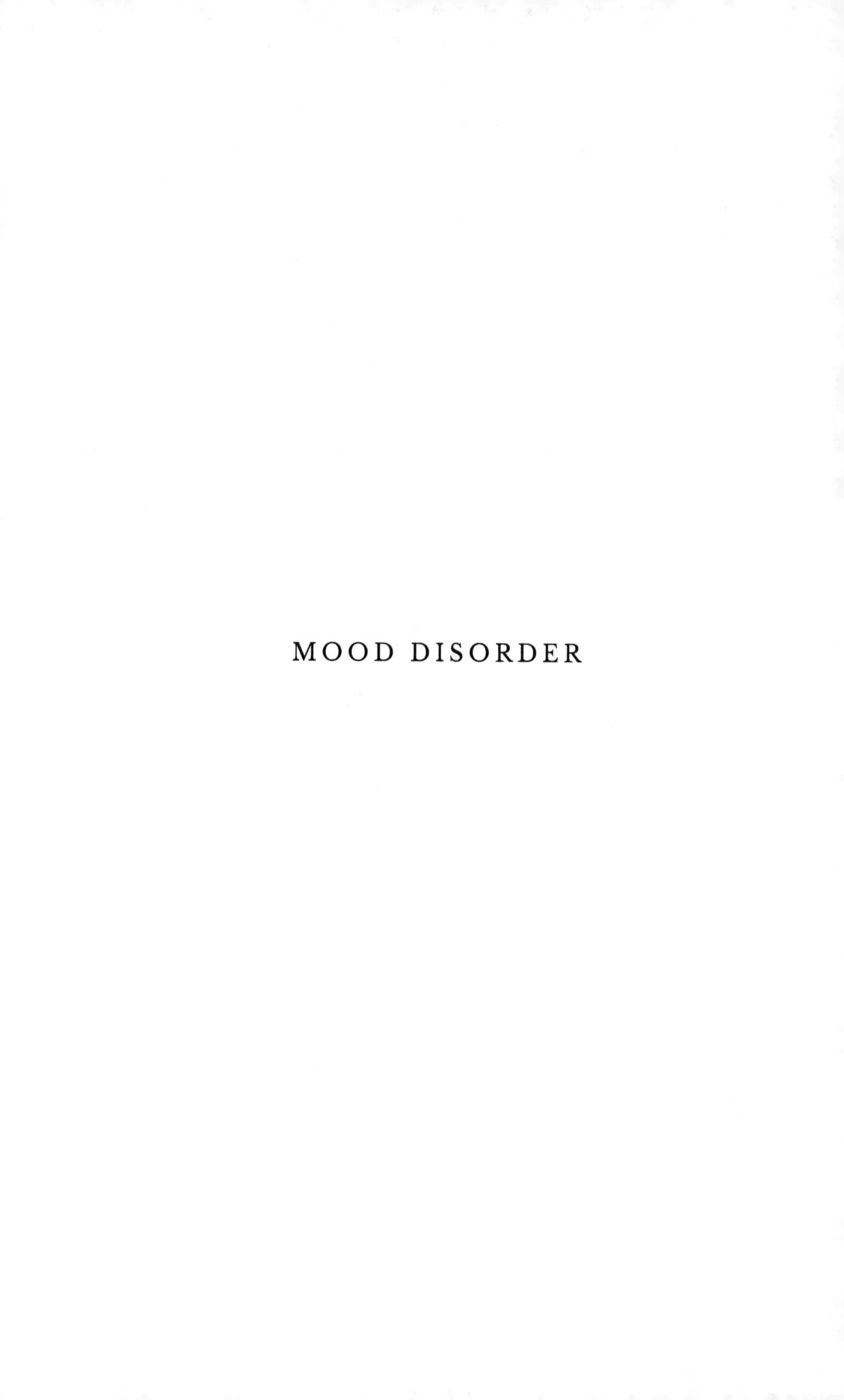

MOOD DISORDER

ANXIETY

All I can hear is my heartbeat

Fast, loud, heavy breathing

Eyes scanning, temperature rising

Palms sweaty

Flight response is high

Panic sets in

The room seems to spin

All I can hear is my heartbeat

Fast fast fast

Waiting for this to pass

It seems unbearable

How long will it last

Eyes scanning, I look for an escape

For a way outside this place

For a way outside this space

Nobody is safe

All I can hear is my heartbeat
My fingers twitch beside me
Body shakes with anxiety
My nausea rises inside of me

                        and
                          I
                            am
                                  not
                        okay

I softly close my eyes
Start counting in my mind
Trying to slow time
And become more aligned
With the voices inside

1...
    2...
        3...

                        I open my eyes to see
                        I inhale deep and breathe
                        I tap my fingers to the beat
                                        1...
                                        2...
                                        3...

I become grounded with my feet

Slow and steady

I change my focus

I listen closely to my body

I breathe in and repeat

1...

   2...

      3...

And all I can hear....

Is my heartbeat

ANXIETY

When I begin to worry about what
tomorrow will bring,
I begin to sweat and my heart begins to
sink
I begin to overthink
My self-confidence begins to shrink
And I start to feel small
And afraid of it all
I shut down and avoid all calls
Responsibility can't find me if I'm curled
up in a ball
And staring at the bedroom wall
I don't have any answers
Please don't ask anything of me
Let me stay here in this moment
Completely void of accountability
Let me spiral as the tears fall from my
cheeks

I don't think I can do this
It all seems too much for me to handle
And as quickly as one blows out a candle
I am lost in everything I'm not and
everything I can't be
Well, this is what happens when I begin
to trust my anxiety

DEPRESSION

I tend to always use the word consume
when I talk about depression
I say the darkness consumes me, but it
doesn't just consume
It envelops me, it wraps me up in its claws
and tears away at my being
It mocks me, laughs at my pain, ensnares
me in its web, and threatens me with its
sting
It takes my breath away making it harder
to breathe,
I trip and fall further into the darkness, it
welcomes me and antagonizes me, brings
me gifts but will not let me leave
It's a contradiction, it invites me in yet
tortures me the longer I stay
And I stay, I don't know any other way

I search for a window, a beam of light,
anything to free me from this room
Everything I see and everywhere I turn,
it's dark, it hurts, and it's hard
Exhaustion creeps in and breaks my
body into shards
Fatigue washes over me and I'm broken
and worn, I'm beaten down, bruised, I'm
in pain, I'm torn
The voices keep screaming and keep
inviting me in, here we are, here we are,
let us in, let us win

The darkness doesn't just consume, it
looms, it glooms, it traps me in a room
Here I am with my thoughts and it's all I
can face
The excruciating pain in myself and the
lack of safety in my space

It's haunting, it's sad, the tears run down
my face
I want out, I want safety but I can't leave
this place
This place is where you belong, this place
is where you stay, I hear them say
Again, again and again, I am in the same
place
Day after day
"It's the only way" murmurs the
amygdala in my brain
The word consume still lingers as the
darkness skims my fingers and tears apart
my skin from outside to within
The medicine keeps the darkness at bay,
but it lurks just around the corner always
there to warn you,

"I'm here another day, another day,
another day."

CONFLICTED

I'm never alone, for no matter what
happens I will always have a home
My mind keeps me safe my mind gives
me what I need,
My mind tortures me and makes it hard
to breathe
Sometimes I can't sleep sometimes I can't
eat
The voices in my head keep telling me
they need me
I remind them that it's them I need
We work in tangent, like a freshly oiled
machine
It doesn't work if it's missing a piece
I've spent so long running away from it
but it always seems to follow
It provides comfort when I feel sorrow

I see worried and conflicted faces

Do they want to help me?

Do they want to erase us?

Is it safe?

Is it dangerous?

Will we ever understand the minds that
plague us?

Or will we ever understand the minds
that save us?

I'm conflicted, I feel more peace than
unease

It's the people who don't seem to
understand me

My mind is a happy place; a safe retreat

My mind also seems to consume me

Without the voices, I can't seem to
breathe

I'm conflicted

When I'm in my darkest place, my mind
keeps me sane
I look for the light as I stare out at the rain
When my body is frozen in fear, my mind
still keeps me safe
I close my eyes and wait for the pain to go
away
I may be hurt, but they give me a reason
to stay
Because of them, my resilience continues
to shine through every single day

I'm never alone, for no matter what
happens I will always have a home
I will always have a place to go, a place to
run to when the highs get too high and the
lows get too low
No matter where I go, I will never be
alone

BIPOLAR

The waves crash high and the tides run
low
I'm soaring upwards with nowhere to go
The fall is inevitable
Sometimes fast
Mostly slow
I feel powerless as the wind tells me
which way to blow
My boundaries crumble as I begin to lose
control
My steady foundation falls into a gaping
hole
I'm left to sink
To question everything I think
Pushed further until I'm on the brink...
Of a breakdown

CAN'T GET OUT OF BED

Today I'm struggling
I pull the sheets higher over me so maybe
I won't be able to breathe
I just want to go back to sleep
But the responsibilities of today beckon
and prod me
I'm overwhelmed
I'm tired of feeling this way
The sanctity of my bed calms me
Why can't I just stay here
Here in these sheets
Resting my head on this cool pillow
As the world moves around me
The sunlight streams into my window
kissing my cheeks
I just want to be here in this moment
I want to be free
Of all burdens and responsibilities

Maybe there's a different way I can
approach it
So it doesn't overwhelm
Maybe there's a way to get out of bed
And to not struggle so much
Isn't the medicine supposed to be helping
with this
The dullness the lack of motivation
The fear of the day and all it brings
I try not to let it win
But today I am struggling
And I am
Going back to sleep

DEPRESSION

A pill a day keeps the voices away
Keeps the stirring thoughts at bay
Keeps me semi-sane I tell myself as I stare
at my reflection in the mirror
My vision is blurred, could it be I don't
recognize my face or is it blurred from
the streaming tears
I don't feel present I don't feel grounded
in this familiar space
I feel detached, lost, out of place,
I stare back into my soul, wishing myself
to remember what it felt like to feel safe
My body is meant to be a vessel, a light, a
story,
I gaze back into my lifeless eyes, and I see
confusion, I feel a lack
A lack of purpose, a lack of love, a lack of
empathy

Where did it go

How could it just disappear

My fists curl, and my tears run deeper

I am sad; infinitely sad,

I am heartbroken; tired of trying to be

good, exhausted with my constant aim of

perfection

The pain persists I try to resist but, the

darkness mocks me and persuades me to

cock my fist,

My hand collides with the glass and I

shatter the mirror, "How do I make

myself disappear" I scream into the

silence

Broken glass riddles my fingers as my

vision runs red

Blood drips from my curled hand and

pools at my feet

Is this me unmedicated?

Is this me free?

But then why is it so hard to breathe?

Why can't I seem to leave?

I hate the reliance on a pill, a promise to
get better but as soon as it's gone, I have
to start over

The idea is cyclic in nature in the way
that it never feels like there's progress

I'm stuck in this repetition of very low
lows and very high highs

I stare down at the broken glass as the
blood heats my fingertips

I can't do any more of this, it can't hurt
this much to simply exist

Is being medicated the answer? Will it
subside this pain?

A pill a day will keep the suicidal
thoughts away I hear my psychiatrist say

Well then maybe I need to be medicated
for just another day

Down the throat, wash it down, done,
goodbye pain for one more day

Maybe I do need to be medicated

WHO AM I

Small tight coils hug my face
Green eyes stare back at me in the mirror
My mouth opens but no sound comes out
Voice silenced for so long, I cannot find it
now
Heart abandoned and broken too many
times to count
Yet still I open my mouth
And try to speak
Maybe someone will hear my whispers for
intimacy no matter how hard I try to push
them away
For fear that their words will strangle and
ensnare me in their false promises and
deceit
I cannot stop trying
Because as soon as I stop fighting, I have
given in and I have given them power

As I stand in this mirror, I stare at this
face staring back at me,
Tears stream down my pale cheeks,
sometimes I do not know who is staring
back at me or where I am meant to be
This life is all I have; this body is all I
own and so many times I do not feel like
it is home
And I feel so confused and alone
I want so much love and to be nurtured, I
want the love I show the angels at my
feet
But it feels like I've had to fight for
someone to show me this love all my life
What did I do wrong? I feel tired and
weak, but I know I cannot admit defeat
I have people and angels that rely on me
Every day I struggle to breathe but I
crack a smile as inside I bleed
Because I do not want them to see the
real me
I am afraid I am not as strong as I may
seem

My body continues to grow weak, and I
still cannot find the words to speak
My inner paranoia continues to creep
And I build higher walls around my bed
so I can feel safer when I sleep
Double-lock the door so the nightmares
will leave
Even though the shadows still follow me
and haunt me in my dreams
Is this how I am supposed to feel, is this
how life's supposed to be?
Hiding in my bathroom and afraid to
speak
What do they all see in me? They say I
have a voice but they don't listen when I
whisper
So, today I hide from their words
because I am not ready to scream
I wipe my tears and smile at the girl
staring back at me
I whisper to the person staring back at
me in the mirror:

"This is your true identity"

A NOTE FROM ME

I can't tell you if everything in the end turns out okay because I haven't met that day and most of the time it doesn't feel that way. I know that today, it seems like it's okay and it seems like you and I might just make it. There are people out there who care and who want you to be here; including me. Please stay here a little longer with me. We can figure this world out together. You don't have to be alone in this. You are not a burden. I'm here to listen. Always.

TRAUMA & ADDICTION

FRAGILITY

One touch is all it takes

To watch me shatter to the floor in pieces

My skin is so easy to break

My fragility keeps the love at bay

Because one gentle touch will cause me to
decay

But the touches are not gentle, fingers are
forced at my throat

Forced at my heart, forced as I choke

And I am still expected to breathe and
have the strength and expected to be an
art piece

My lips quiver as I gasp for air, I curl into
my body afraid of it all

Afraid of those I love, afraid of the pain
they inflict

Where am I to find strength when this is
what I have been reduced to?
A fragile piece of art that no one wants to
look at, no one wants to see
I tell myself if I close my eyes then
everyone will leave
And the fingers wrapped around my
throat will cease
And my pain will decrease
But they won't leave, they won't let me be
They take advantage of the fragility and
wait until all I do is bleed
They rip my tongue out so I won't speak
and squeeze harder on my neck so I won't
breathe
Then I am asked to give all of me, as I
bleed, as I lay weak
I can't ask for anything in return, my love
is all they seek,
My frail body lies slumped over, blood
pooled at my mouth and feet,
They whisper in my ear, "Your love is all I
have, your love will set me free"

I hear the footsteps then recede as I am
left to recover and seek strength
I lay here, a fragile piece of art, that no
one wants to look at and no one wants to
see

TRAUMA

Cold fingers pry at my skin,
They start to take and consume without
my consent
My heart pounds and my breath shallows
Dissociation takes over and I am
rendered speechless
I am not safe here I tell myself but there's
nothing I can do
The hands continue to search and seek
out vulnerability and weakness
My fear entraps me and destabilizes my
being
Someone, please help me,
Can anyone see me, can anyone hear me
My mouth opens but I cannot speak
But what can I do, what can I say?
To make the hands stop and go away?
I just want to be okay
I want to feel safe

Who has stolen the words from my tongue
Who has bound my wrists and rendered me
immobile
Water floods my brain as I lose myself in
learned helplessness
I shut my eyelids tight, if I can't see
anything, is it still happening?
What happens when the hands stop prying,
they stop grabbing, they stop hurting
How am I supposed to process how much
has been taken from me
My security my well-being, my sense of
safety?
Then I'm expected to feel safe and secure in
new surroundings with new hands
New hands that still can pry and consume
Hands that can grab and take more of me
Hands that can bind my wrists and
immobilize me
Tell me, how can I ever feel safe again when
these were hands I trusted to keep me safe

ADDICTION

I feel numb
Drugs started feeling like it's decaf
Inject swallow snort
Lying down staring at the bare ceiling
wondering why it doesn't work
No, I don't want help
No, I don't want rehab
I just want to be in this moment
I just want to feel bad
Positivity exudes through me but it's a
learned characteristic
Enduring the pain and all the abuse has
made me insane
But you can't let them know you're
melting away
Into nothingness or into something
So you adapt

You're a sane person,

a figment of your imagination

An apparition

But to them, a solid foundation

Built on a learned smile and fake laugh

... an inspiration

To not lose my mind...damn

I lost all concept of time

So teeth are clenched and the sadness is

quenched

And the heart and mind get drenched

In a wave of adaptation

And I am trapped inside a fence, where I

am scared to leave

... and they are scared to enter

ADOPTION

Small fingers reach upward connecting

with empty air

Confusion sets in,

They aren't there

They aren't anywhere

Not there to kiss your scrapes,

Not there to brush your hair

Each day unfamiliarity is thrust upon

you

Aggressive hands, aggressive voices,

Angry whispers, hushed shouts

You open your mouth but no words

come out

Food and a bed aren't promised

Comfort has lost all its glow

As you continue to be the topic of

conversation of people you don't know

You had dreams and goals
You were going to master coloring in the
lines
And being comfortable with the unknown
Now there isn't enough time
Each day you are being ripped away from
the ones who cared
Why aren't they there,
You look around but you can't find them
anywhere
Do they not care?
You have so much to share,
Will you see them again?
This feels like a lot for you to bear,
Unknown arms reach down to displace
you
They turn and face you
They say they will kiss your scrapes
They will brush your hair
But you don't care
You look around one more time,
They still aren't there
They aren't anywhere

PROTECTION

Every day I build walls
Walls that will deter them all
Laying each brick by brick, my tears flow
This was not how it was supposed to go
Now I'm in too deep and the barriers are
too high
The walls are thick, no one can pry
No one can get inside, no one can try
Up, up, up, level after level,
Brick after brick, I lay them down and
quick
No one can penetrate these walls,
I'd like to see them try
Curled up inside I look up and cry
The perimeter gets higher as the days go
by

I'm tired, tired of people taking all of me until
there is nothing left
Every single time, I scream as my cheeks are
stained wet
I'm tired of giving and never receiving
I'm tired of people getting all they need and
leaving
So back to the laying of the bricks
Back to the safe walls that hold me in
Back to shutting down, back to letting people
win
I can't do this anymore, I can't keep getting hurt
again and again
It's suffocating, it's nauseating, it's tearing me
from within
Every day I build walls
Walls that will deter them all
Laying brick after brick, I feel so alone
But these walls are my safety, these walls are my
home

A NOTE FROM ME

"At this moment in my body I am safe, I am loved, I am here, I am okay."
Just for this moment.
Trust me, I know the feelings are hard and they overwhelm and seem to persist.
Just breathe.
At this moment, you are okay, and you are still here.

LOVED LOST & LONGING

LONGING

You calm me with just one look
A look deep into my soul healing my
inner wounds
My face flushes, my heart racing, palms
clench
All the unspoken words linger on my lips
Fear of losing everything gets the better
of me and I stay silent
There is a battle inside with each look in
my eyes
An unwinnable war
I can't shake this feeling, I can't run from
it
It twists my soul and I'm at its mercy
My breath stills, my insides shake as I try
to compose myself

I cling to an irrational shimmer of hope
knowing deep down there's nothing left
but the memories of our love
Castaway in the sea is everything that
reminds us of what once was
I reach out towards the crashing waves to
try and find a glimpse of you
But I am met with nothing else but the
chaotic waves of blue
I turn away and drop down in the sand
Exhaustion hits me as I continue to hide
from the bitter truth
I'm still completely in love with you

MEMORIES AT SEA

How fast does time fly
Onto the wings of a bird as it flutters by
It seems like just yesterday, you were in
my life
Holding my hand
Holding it tight
I told myself you would never let it go
But that's exactly what you did
How could I have ever known?
Years pass by and I am left with the
memories
It's all that's shown
You used to tell me you loved me
We used to share a home

Now you're gone and my future with you
is fleeting
The amount of time we still have in each
other's lives is unknown
Where did the time go?
Washed away at sea
Along with the love you held for me
You let go of my hand as soon as the
waves got too high
And the water became too deep
Now all that is left are the memories I
keep
When it was just you and me holding
hands
As tight as we would need
I miss you but I miss more what we used
to be
But that time is gone
Caught on the wings of a bird
Flying high above the sea I lost you in

JUST BE FRIENDS

I steal a glance in your direction
Feelings of overwhelming sadness wash
over my heart
You took a piece of it when you left
Now you're sitting next to me with my
heart in your hands
I don't know what to think or expect
I don't know where to sit or where I stand
I sit next to you watching a piece of my
heart bleed out
Blood dripping in between your fingers

My breath catches

My gaze lingers

I look down at the piece of yours I hold

delicately in my hand

I blink tears away

I try to rise above these waves so I don't

drown

I used to know what to do in this

situation but the smoke has my head in

the clouds

Another inhale

Another gaze

Another grin

As I laugh I think to myself

I don't know if we can just be friends

REST IN PEACE

When I think of death, I think
"How can one simply not exist?"
Then I curse myself for sometimes having
that wish
I know one's soul lives on
But it's so hard to be strong
When you cannot hear their voice
You can't be held in their arms where you
belong
Where do you go?
Where do you stay?
Besides in my heart and thoughts each
day

I know everyone will experience this too
someday
And sometimes I am met with fear
Other times, I feel just okay
It heightens the importance of
cherishing one's life for me
I began to love more and embrace life's
beauty
Because at the end of it all
I never want anyone to say
They didn't get to see all of me
And everything I could be

REST IN PEACE

With each step, your little paws would
follow
So much happiness in each and every wag
of your tail
You will always be my yesterday, today,
and tomorrow
Your unconditional love will always be
my ship's sail
Please carry me to a land where hearts
don't break and there is an absence of
sorrow

Over the bridge splashed in vibrant
colors, we will travel
Tears stream down my cheeks;
I know this isn't an easy journey
My palms are sweaty and my emotions
begin to unravel

My knuckles turn white as I try to hold on
to more than just the memories of you
I beg my body to keep traveling, I know I
can make it through,
But I just don't want to ever live a life
without you,

You were my best friend, my heart, my
soul, my everything
You were there for me on the days there
was sun and on the days when there was
only rain
You stared into my soul and healed every
wound and pain
You have changed my life in each and
every single way,
You have taken my heart, and forever
with you it will stay

I travel across this rainbow bridge and I
pray,
that I will see my best friend again
someday

Because with each step now, your little
paws still follow,
And the love that you showed me is what
keeps me walking into yesterday, today,
and tomorrow

I love you,
I will see you again soon

PLEASE DON'T GO

My heart sinks

My chest tightens

My breathing shallows

As I think about a future with you, not in it

Tears well at the corner of my eyes as I feel a

magnitude of sorrow

Wash over me

Each waking day I spend with you and

You are always right there to quell the pain and

the loneliness

I stare into your eyes begging you to stay

Stay forever here with me

You are everything

All of it and me

When I am with you I become saddened when

I realize one day you won't be here

You won't exist on this earth

I can't understand how one day you're here

and the next, you dissipate into thin air

My heart sinks

My chest tightens

My breathing shallows

As I think about a world without you

How will I cope?

How can I help you stay?

I can't do this

Is there any other way I beg and plead

I cannot breathe

You are a piece of me and one day you'll
just leave

Leaving me with nothing but memories
and grief

As I hold you in my arms

All I can do is just be

And cherish our times together,

Just you and me

Please don't go

Please don't leave

A NOTE FROM ME

You are meant to be here. I know the pain can be unbearable and it seems to consume and loom. I promise you, you are meant to be here on this earth. I understand feeling utterly alone, feeling as if I am nothing. I understand feeling like a burden, feeling as if my time here has been a waste. And I promise you, you are not a burden, you are worthy of love and safety. Please, stay on this earth. You are meant to be here.

PART II

FINDING THE LIGHT

"Only when we are brave enough to explore the darkness will we discover the infinite power of our light." — Brené Brown

SELF LOVE

MEANT TO BE

As the flower needs the bee,

You are meant to be

Like a leaf on a tree,

You are meant to be

As the sky meets the sea,

You are meant to be

You have a purpose,

You are meant to be

Please stay a little longer on this earth

with me

INNER PEACE

Warm water rains on my bare skin

Inhale...exhale... I feel alive again

Cold air kisses my fresh skin

Inhale...exhale...I feel anew again

Fluffy blanket cocoons around my
body

Inhale... exhale...I feel comforted again

Sunlight flirts with my window pane

Inhale...exhale...I feel light again

My plants dance with the sunbeams

Inhale...exhale... I feel growth again

My dogs curl up around my feet

Inhale... exhale... I feel safe again

A smile plays on my lips

Keep me in this moment

Inhale...exhale...

Keep me safe

Inhale... exhale...

Keep me cozy

REST

Lofi beats stream through the room
My eyes close and I take in a deep breath and
exhale
Today I choose rest
I need to be gentle with my body
I need inner peace
I want to feel as if I'm floating down a stream
Fingers dancing through the trickling water
Eyes towards the bright blue sky
Searching for shapes in the clouds as they drift
by
The music tickles my ears and I begin to soften
My limbs seep into the cool sheets
As I'm surrounded by the fresh cotton
I let go of all the worries as I take the time to
rest and unwind
They don't go very far though
Their time will come
But for now,
I choose to rest my body and my mind in this
calm morning

INNER CHILD

My inner child has a voice
She speaks steadily and slowly so those
listening can hear and understand
Will you listen?
Will you accept her outstretched hand?
Will you answer her when she calls?
Alone in her bed, the demons creep
The darkness around her looms as they
curl their fingers around her sheets
"Where are you"
She silently screams

As fear terrorizes her entire being and
robs her of a peaceful sleep
She squeezes her eyes tight
Praying the darkness leaves her for just
one night
She wants a hug and comfort
Someone to remind her this is temporary
and not permanent
But she looks around and no one is here
Just the darkness, demons, and the fear
No one is here to wipe away the tears
And remind her that daylight is near
She prays one day someone will come but
years go by
And she's still on her own even in her own
home
Her nightlight helps when the darkness
begins to roam
She didn't think she asked for much
Just comfort and a hug when times were
tough
Just for someone to show her some love

Her voice was slow and steady so they
would listen
"But no one was there," she tells herself
as her eyes begin to glisten
So she nurtures and hugs her inner child
when she cries
She holds her hand,
Wipes her tears,
And becomes her light
Because it's never too late to listen
It's never too late to grab her
outstretched hand
It's never too late to show her you love
her
And to calm her fears at night
To my inner child:
I love you and you deserve the world.
You are worthy of love; let's heal
together.

IT'S THE LITTLE THINGS

It's the little things
That help me get by
The joy swells within my chest
And my breath exhales into a sigh
It's the rain pouring down on the
pavement
It's the wind blowing through the trees
The leaves catching the raindrops
It's the flowers relaxing in the rain
I stare out the window and I feel whole
again
It's the little things that help me get by
It's the time spent doing the things I
love
The alone time to allow for
rejuvenation
I recharge in the peace
I recharge for me
For my sanity and happiness

It's the little things that help get me by
Spending time cuddling in bed with the animals I
love
Feeling the cool side of my pillow and the warm
blankets wrapped around my body
It's the sweet melodies of the songs I love
And the birds singing outside my window
Without a care in the world
It's being around the people I adore
It's allowing me new experiences and new realms
of nature to explore
It's allowing myself to rest when my body can't do
anymore
It's buying myself flowers from the nearby
grocery store
And placing them in a tiny vase next to my
window
It's the rising of the dough as I bake biscuits in the
kitchen feeling the heat from my stove
It's the little things that help me stay another day
The colored pencils surround me as I carefully fill
in my coloring book
It's the yarn I use to stitch my designs
It's the utter joy that books give me as I read each
line

It's the wagging tails as I walk my dogs in
the sunshine after the rain
It's the way I move across the room
dancing in beat to my favorite tune
It's the feeling of being utterly alone and at
peace in my room
It's the feeling of reading by candlelight as
I sit under the light of the moon
It's the little things that help me be here
another day
The little things that add more laughter
and joy to my day
It's the little things when the world feels
like a scary place and I feel like I'm not
okay
It's the little things when the tears are
demanding to stay streaming down my
face
It's the little things when I tell myself I
can't stay another day

I do the little things that help me stay here
To remind myself and others that the little
things will always be here
Find the little things to help you get by
Find the little things that bring joy into
your life
The little things that help you fall in love
with your life again,
You can make it another day, remember
it's the little things.

THE GARDEN

Flowers began to sprout up where weeds once
spread amongst the garden
Something so beautiful can rise from destruction
Seeds were planted in the desolate waste
The sun shined
The water flowed
And the land began to grow
Something anew was sown
Sprouting hope throughout the weary soil
A new foundation laid
The land laughs and cries
It soaks up the darkness and the light
A garden once dismissed begins to emerge and
shine
New roots become intertwined in the vines
Emotions are embraced
Tears roll off the petals of fresh flowers
The leaves sigh and breathe with each ebb and
flow

The grass tickles my feet as I make my way

I run my fingers through the fresh soil

My tears sustain the new life

I am glad I stayed here

I am reminded that where there is light, there is always

hope

There is always growth

as I sit in my garden

I can feel the sun on my skin

The warmth rising within

Becoming one with the earth

I have found my worth

I lay down and let the flowers grow around me

I have become the garden

and the garden has become me

SHINE ON ME

Twinkle sparkle and shine

Her growth has become defined

Her soul has become divine

And wisdom flows through her body and mind

Oh what a brilliant time

To have her hand in mine

As the trellis holds the vine

The music ascends

And the clock tells time

We dance under the shadows cast by candlelight

There's beauty in the darkness that now shines so
bright

SPIRTUALITY

INNER PEACE

Take me to my happy place
Where the wind teases my hair
And the sunbeams kiss my face
Take me to my happy place
Where I gently close my eyes
And all the painful thoughts erase
Take me to my happy place
Where I can channel my inner child
Where I can run and I can play
Take me somewhere new
With the clouds painted in the sky
Amidst a sea of bright blue
Let me run my fingers through the grass
Praying I can stay here
Praying that this will last

Take my hand and lead me

Help me find my peace

As I find myself becoming who I want to

be

Hold me in your arms

As we dance across the sea

It's just you and me

And endless depths of blue as far as our

eyes can see

Take me to my happy place

This is where I want to stay

This is where I want to be

Sitting next to you as we stare out at the

sea

THE DANCE

The fear comes at night
It comes bearing darkness
Completely void of light
It comes to kill and destroy
I crawl further under the sheets until I
can feel safe again
I pray for strength and peace as my tears
fall onto my cheeks
Then you appear with an outstretched
hand
Ready to protect and cast away the fear
I take your hand with trembling fingers
My heart pounding in my chest

You take the lead and I follow you
through the dark abyss
Shining a light with each rhythmic step
With every movement, you bring
comfort and safety as we glide across the
room
Steps here
Steps there
You handle me with soft care
I know in my heart you are always there
We waltz across the room moving in time
with ease
Your grace and light brighten the room
and pace flows through me like cascading
waves
Fear subsides as you hold me

.

You call me worthy even when I feel
like a burden
You soothe my soul as we dance
With you, I know I am safe
With you, I know I have a chance
To make it through the night
Thank you for this dance and thank you
for this light
I will see you again tomorrow night

.

THE SWING

Streams of water cascade down the
marble
As the wind chime whispers hello
An array of majestic colors paints a
picture across the lush valley
The flowers dance as the wind blows
There is peace in this moment
No anxiety about the unknown
My heart beats a sigh of relief
How can I make this feeling my forever
home
How can I reach out and capture this
moment
How can I savor something so precious
and fleeting
Tell me I can channel this peace
Give me life
Give me meaning

The water gently kisses the marble
The birds flutter by on swift wings
The whispers of the chime put my mind
at ease
As I sit here on this metal swing
Back and forth I rock
As the wind tickles the grass
And the birds begin to sing
The tree branches sway in tune
As Mother Nature begins to breathe
Help me hold onto this peace, the
present, the meaning
I just want to be okay
Even for a moment give me some
reprieve
I sigh, close my eyes, and listen to the
streams of water cascade down the
marble
As I sit here on this metal swing

AFFECTION

DARLING

Like a gentle breeze in the night please carry
me with you wherever you go.
Nurture and provide as the flowers bloom
and the fields grow
Gently touch the scars that adorn my body
Reminders of a past self who I no longer
know
Darling, am I safe here? Where did you go?
Am I able to trust you? Can we go slow?
Can you feel my heartbeat through your
fingertips
Can you look me in the eyes as my name
falls from your lips
My heart has been ready for a moment like
this
I gaze into your eyes as the lights dance
across the room
We are two different souls
I attract the sun and you attract the moon.
Please tell me, darling, are we falling in love
too soon?

VULNERABLE

Fragile skin
Tender lashes sweep my cheeks
I am overcome with vulnerability
What is it that draws you
What do you see in me
Tell me what drives your sheer
curiosity
Safety has always been an issue in my
body
Quivering lips and halted breath
I flex my hands and fingertips,
I sense the power in you

In the things you say
And the things you do
And the way I feel about you
How can I get closer to your soul
Is this real or how will I know
My body shivers and I want to let go
I am not used to being protected and
being cared for
And all I ask of you is to wipe my tears
when I cry and stick by my side
Well maybe I am asking more of you
because I want more of you
Will you wrap me in your arms
And protect me from all harm

SHOW ME

Show me a human who loves me like my dog
loves me with the utmost support and who
loves me unconditionally
How easy is it to love and forgive as easily as
the waves ebb and flow into the sea
Show me someone who soothes my soul with
one look in the eye as my head is in my hands
and as I curl up and cry
Please show me
Show me who will ever take their place when
they are removed from my life on their final
days
Tell me how they can say it all without ever
having to speak yet I listen to people who will
talk for hours and say nothing of meaning
Give me someone who teaches me every single
day the beauty of life and gives me all the
reasons to stay
Show me an angel who can give me life and
hope just by standing on four feet

I see the world in their eyes yet I cannot
provide it for them
So I'll do my best to give these little
angels the love they deserve until they
reach the final chapter on this earth
And then they ascend to where they
belong.
Forever they will be; my paw prints in
heaven, walking right along

.

IN THE DARKNESS

Every time I want to leave, you illuminate a
new path for me
What will become of me when you're not here
I will have to find another source of light I fear
Intense sorrow grips my heart
To think someday soon we must part
I've been told I can't rely on you to be my hope
and my identity
It's a lot of uncontrollable pressure on you
from me
I try not to but sometimes you are the only
hope I see
When the world seems to tune me out
You are the only ones who take the time to
listen
I never feel alone and I never feel like I don't
have a voice
I can't comprehend the loss I'll feel when
you're no longer here

When you're no longer in my space
When you're no longer near
I know I don't have a choice

Your unconditional love is such a
blessing and I'll cherish it for as long as
I have on this earth
You have given me light, hope, and a
voice
You are my lights in the darkness
You help me see
Please stay here as long as you can with
me

.

MENTAL HEALTH
RESOURCES

SUICIDE & CRISIS HOTLINE
CALL/TEXT 988
CHAT @ 988LIFELINE.ORG

NATIONAL ASSOCIATION OF MENTAL ILLNESS HOTLINE (NAMI)

TEXT "HELPLINE" TO 62640

CALL NAMI HELPLINE 800-950-6264 (NAMI)
FIND RESOURCES @ NAMI.ORG/HELP

NATIONAL SEXUAL ASSAULT HOTLINE:
CALL 800-656-4673 (HOPE)

NATIONAL DOMESTIC VIOLENCE HOTLINE:
CALL 800-799-7233 (SAFE)